Smoothies
Cocktails
Juices

Smoothies
Cocktails
Juices

Frances Mayfield

p

This is a Parragon Book
This edition published in 2006

Parragon
Queen Street House
4 Queen Street
Bath BA1 1HE, UK

ISBN: 1-40547-197-2

Printed in China

Produced by the Bridgewater Book Company Ltd.

Cover by Talking Design

Additional photography: Calvey Taylor-Haw

Notes for the Reader

This book uses both metric and imperial measurements. Follow the same units of
measurement throughout; do not mix metric and imperial. All spoon measurements are
level: teaspoons are assumed to be 5 ml, and tablespoons are assumed to be 15 ml.
Unless otherwise stated, milk is assumed to be full fat, eggs and individual fruits
such as bananas are medium and pepper is freshly ground black pepper.

Recipes using raw or very lightly cooked eggs should be avoided by infants, the elderly,
pregnant women, convalescents and anyone suffering from an illness.

Contents

Introduction

And the lilies of your arms are beckoning me
O my summer garden

Guillaume Apollinaire *The Ninth Secret Poem*
Translated by Oliver Bernard

Few things in life are as idyllic as relaxing in the garden on a lazy, hot
summer's day with a cooling summer drink, whether you prefer a breakfast
fruit smoothie, an afternoon iced tea, a cocktail-hour margarita or all three.
Many of these recipes include fruit and are a great way of drinking summer's
wonderful harvest, as well as counting towards your recommended five daily
portions of fruit and vegetables. By choosing the raw ingredients, you can also
make your drinks organic if you want. The classic, frozen and summer cocktails
will kick-start any summer party, while there are also plenty of delicious non-
alcoholic thirst quenchers and iced substitutes for tea and coffee.

Equipment

Many of the recipes require a food processor. You can use a blender instead, but the blenders used behind bars are pretty robust, so check first that yours is suitable. A juicer is another valuable piece of equipment, and freshly squeezed juices will take your drinks to a new level.

❖ For the cocktails you will need a mixing glass or jug to mix together stirred cocktails, and a cocktail shaker or blender to blend shaken cocktails.

❖ In the recipes we have listed the alcohol in 'measures'. A measure is a bar measure, equivalent to one jigger or 25 ml/1 fl oz. If you don't have a jigger, use the measures as a guide to get the proportions right.

Blending drinks

Stirred drinks simply require you to pour the juices or alcohol over a glass half-filled with cracked ice. Stir with a long-handled spoon. Then, if stated in the recipe, strain into another glass to prevent the ice diluting the drink. When using a cocktail shaker, the drink is ready when a 'frost' forms. This is the condensation that will appear on the metal shaker after about 10–20 seconds.

Glasses

For most drinks, any glass is suitable, though a sturdy, tall glass is good for a thick shake or smoothie. Classic cocktails are often served in a specified glass, indicated in the recipe, but tumblers and wine glasses can cover most needs. Chill your glasses in the freezer for 10 minutes before serving to keep drinks chilled and frosty.

Ice

Summer drinks need to be ice-cold and it's worth keeping a bag of ice in the freezer. Cracked ice is made by placing cubes in a polythene bag and hitting them against a wall or crushing with a rolling pin. Crushed ice for blended drinks is made in the same way but broken up into much smaller pieces. If you have a powerful food processor or blender you can crack or crush the ice with this, but check the manufacturer's instructions first so you don't damage the blades.

❖ For fruit drinks, freeze the fruit first. Fruit can be processed straight from frozen, and with berries or pineapple chunks in your freezer you can create a taste of summer whatever the season.

Decorations

For fruit drinks, the best decoration is just a handful or wedge of the fruit. Berries can be speared on to cocktail sticks and hung over the glass; wedges of fruit cut and slipped on to the rim. Cocktails often have classic decorations, such as the olive in a martini, and glasses can be frosted with sugar or salt by rubbing the rim with juice, then dipping into a saucer of sugar or salt.

Sweetening your drinks

Many summer drinks need a little sweetening, but because they are cold there is nothing to dissolve the sugar. You can buy bottles of sugar syrup or make it yourself by stirring an equal amount of water and caster sugar in a small saucepan over a low heat until the sugar dissolves. Bring to the boil and simmer for a few minutes, then cool. Refrigerate and use within 2 weeks.

smoothies
& juices

Cranberry Sunrise

❖ Pour the cranberry juice and orange juice into a food processor and process gently until combined. Add the raspberries and lemon juice and process until smooth. ❖ Pour the mixture into glasses and decorate with slices and spirals of lemon or orange. Serve at once.

SERVES 2

300 ml/10 fl oz cranberry juice
100 ml/3½ fl oz orange juice
150 g/5½ oz raspberries
1 tbsp lemon juice

TO DECORATE
slices and spirals of lemon
or orange

Forest Fruit Smoothie

SERVES 2

350 ml/12 fl oz orange juice
1 banana, peeled, sliced
  and frozen
450 g/1 lb frozen forest fruits
  (such as blueberries,
  raspberries and blackberries)

TO DECORATE
slices of strawberry

❖ Pour the orange juice into a food processor. Add the banana and half of the forest fruits and process until smooth. ❖ Add the remaining forest fruits and process until smooth. Pour the mixture into tall glasses and decorate the rims with slices of strawberry. Add straws and serve.

O my Luve's like a red, red rose,
That's newly sprung in June

Robert Burns *A Red, Red Rose*

Coconut Cream

❖ Pour the pineapple juice and coconut milk into a food processor. Add the ice cream and process until smooth.
❖ Add the pineapple chunks and process until smooth. Pour the mixture into scooped-out coconut shells, or tall glasses, and decorate with grated fresh coconut. Add straws and serve.

SERVES 2

350 ml/12 fl oz pineapple juice
90 ml/3¼ fl oz coconut milk
150 g/5½ oz vanilla ice cream
140 g/5 oz frozen
pineapple chunks

TO DECORATE
2 tbsp grated fresh coconut

SMOOTHIES & JUICES

Melon Refresher

250 ml/9 fl oz natural yogurt
100 g/3½ oz galia melon,
  skinned and cut into chunks
100 g/3½ oz cantaloupe melon,
  skinned and cut into chunks
100 g/3½ oz watermelon,
  skinned and cut into chunks
6 crushed ice cubes

TO DECORATE
wedges of melon

❖ Pour the yogurt into a food processor. Add the galia melon chunks and process until smooth. ❖ Add the cantaloupe and watermelon chunks along with the crushed ice cubes and process until smooth. Pour the mixture into glasses and decorate with wedges of melon. Serve at once.

Orange & Strawberry Cream

❖ Pour the natural and strawberry
yogurts into a food processor and
process gently. Add the orange juice and
process until combined. ❖ Add the
strawberries and banana and process
until smooth. Pour the mixture into tall
glasses and decorate with slices of
orange and whole strawberries. Add
straws and serve.

SERVES 2

125 ml/4 fl oz natural yogurt
175 ml/6 fl oz strawberry yogurt
175 ml/6 fl oz orange juice
175 g/6 oz frozen strawberries
1 banana, peeled, sliced
and frozen

TO DECORATE
slices of orange
whole fresh strawberries

Summer Fruit Slush

SERVES 2

4 tbsp orange juice
1 tbsp lime juice
100 ml/3½ fl oz sparkling water
350 g/12 oz frozen summer
  fruits (such as blueberries,
  raspberries, blackberries and
  strawberries)
4 crushed ice cubes

TO DECORATE
whole fresh raspberries
whole fresh blackberries

❖ Pour the orange juice, lime juice and sparkling water into a food processor and process gently until combined.
❖ Add the summer fruits and crushed ice cubes and process until a slushy consistency has been reached. ❖ Pour the mixture into glasses, decorate with whole raspberries and blackberries speared on cocktail sticks and serve.

Mango &
Coconut Smoothie

❖ Cut the mangoes in half and remove the stones. Cut away the skin and roughly chop the flesh. ❖ Place the chopped flesh in a food processor with the icing sugar and blend until completely smooth. ❖ Add the coconut milk and crushed ice cubes to the food processor and blend again until frothy. ❖ Pour into tall glasses and sprinkle with toasted flaked coconut to serve.

SERVES 4

2 large, ripe mangoes
1 tbsp icing sugar
500 ml/18 fl oz coconut milk
5 crushed ice cubes

TO DECORATE
flaked coconut, toasted

Pineapple Tango

125 ml/4 fl oz pineapple juice
juice of 1 lemon
100 ml/3½ fl oz water
3 tbsp brown sugar
175 ml/6 fl oz natural yogurt
1 peach, peeled, cut into
  chunks and frozen
100 g/3½ oz frozen
  pineapple chunks

TO DECORATE
wedges of fresh pineapple

❖ Pour the pineapple juice, lemon juice and water into a food processor. Add the sugar and yogurt and process until blended. ❖ Add the peach and pineapple chunks and process until smooth. Pour the mixture into glasses and decorate the rims with wedges of pineapple. Serve at once.

Melon & Pineapple Slush

❖ Pour the pineapple juice and orange juice into a food processor and process gently until combined. ❖ Add the melon, pineapple chunks and crushed ice cubes and process until a slushy consistency has been reached. ❖ Pour the mixture into glasses and decorate with slices of melon and orange. Serve at once.

*'Tis now the summer
of your youth*

Edward Moore *The Gamester*

SERVES 2

100 ml/3½ fl oz
pineapple juice
4 tbsp orange juice
125 g/4½ oz galia melon,
skinned and cut into chunks
140 g/5 oz frozen
pineapple chunks
4 crushed ice cubes

TO DECORATE
slices of galia melon
slices of orange

Vegan Tropical Smoothie

100 ml/3½ fl oz coconut milk
200 ml/7 fl oz soya milk
100 ml/3½ fl oz pineapple juice
1 tbsp brown sugar
1 ripe mango, peeled, stoned
  and diced
2 tbsp grated fresh coconut
140 g/5 oz pineapple chunks
1 banana, peeled, sliced and
  frozen

TO DECORATE
grated fresh coconut
wedges of fresh pineapple

❖ Put the coconut milk, soya milk, pineapple juice and sugar into a food processor and process gently until combined. Add the diced mango to the food processor along with the grated coconut and process well. ❖ Add the pineapple chunks and banana and process until smooth. Pour the mixture into glasses, scatter over some grated fresh coconut and decorate the rims with wedges of pineapple. Serve at once.

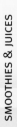

Carrot & Red Pepper Booster

❖ Pour the carrot juice and tomato juice into a food processor and process gently until combined. ❖ Add the red peppers and lemon juice. Season with plenty of freshly ground black pepper and process until smooth. Pour the mixture into tall glasses, add straws and serve.

SERVES 2

250 ml/9 fl oz carrot juice
250 ml/9 fl oz tomato juice
2 large red peppers, deseeded
and roughly chopped
1 tbsp lemon juice
freshly ground black pepper

cocktails

Stinger

❖ Put the cracked ice cubes into a cocktail shaker. Pour the brandy and crème de menthe over the ice. Shake vigorously until a frost forms. ❖ Strain into a small, chilled highball glass.

SERVES 1

4–6 cracked ice cubes
2 measures brandy
1 measure white crème de menthe

The way to ensure summer in England is to have it framed and glazed in a comfortable room

Horace Walpole *Letter to William Cole*

American Rose

SERVES 1

4–6 cracked ice cubes
1½ measures brandy
1 tsp grenadine
½ tsp Pernod
½ peach, peeled and mashed
sparkling wine, to top up

TO DECORATE
wedge of peach

❖ Put the cracked ice cubes into a cocktail shaker. Pour the brandy, grenadine and Pernod over the ice and add the peach. Shake vigorously until a frost forms. ❖ Strain into a chilled wine goblet, top up with sparkling wine and stir. Decorate with a wedge of peach.

*'Tis the last rose of summer
Left blooming alone*

Thomas Moore *'Tis the Last Rose*

Old-fashioned

❖ Put the sugar cube into a small, chilled old-fashioned glass. Dash the bitters over the cube and add the water. Mash with a spoon until the sugar has dissolved.

❖ Pour the bourbon into the glass and stir. Add the cracked ice cubes and decorate with a twist of lemon rind.

SERVES 1

1 sugar cube
dash of Angostura bitters
1 tsp water
2 measures bourbon
or rye whiskey
4–6 cracked ice cubes

TO DECORATE
twist of lemon rind

Manhattan

SERVES 1

4–6 cracked ice cubes
dash of Angostura bitters
3 measures rye whiskey
1 measure sweet vermouth

TO DECORATE

cocktail cherry

❖ Put the cracked ice cubes into a mixing glass. Dash the Angostura bitters over the ice and pour in the whiskey and vermouth. Stir well to mix. ❖ Strain into a chilled glass and decorate with a cocktail cherry.

Mint Julep

❖ Put the mint leaves and Sugar Syrup into a small, chilled glass and mash with a teaspoon. Add crushed ice cubes to fill the glass, then add the bourbon.

❖ Decorate with a sprig of fresh mint.

SERVES 1

leaves of 1 fresh mint sprig
1 tbsp Sugar Syrup
(see page 9)
6–8 crushed ice cubes
3 measures bourbon whiskey

TO DECORATE
sprig of fresh mint

Martini

SERVES 1

4–6 cracked ice cubes
3 measures gin
1 tsp dry vermouth, or to taste

TO DECORATE
cocktail olive

❖ Put the cracked ice cubes into a mixing glass. Pour the gin and vermouth over the ice and stir well to mix.

❖ Strain into a chilled martini glass and decorate with a cocktail olive.

Now welcome, Somer, with thy sonne softe,
·That hast this wintres wedres overshake,
And driven away the longe nyghtes blake!

Geoffrey Chaucer *The Parliament of Fowls*

Orange Blossom

❖ Put the cracked ice cubes into a
cocktail shaker. Pour the gin and orange
juice over the ice and shake vigorously
until a frost forms. ❖ Strain into a chilled
cocktail glass and decorate with a slice
of orange.

SERVES 1

4–6 cracked ice cubes
2 measures gin
2 measures orange juice

TO DECORATE
slice of orange

Alexander

4–6 cracked ice cubes
1 measure gin
1 measure crème de cacao
1 measure single cream

TO DECORATE

freshly grated nutmeg

❖ Put the cracked ice cubes into a cocktail shaker. Pour the gin, crème de cacao and single cream over the ice. Shake vigorously until a frost forms.

❖ Strain into a chilled cocktail glass and sprinkle with the nutmeg.

White Lady

❖ Put the ice cubes into a cocktail shaker. Pour the gin, triple sec and lemon juice over the ice. Shake vigorously until a frost forms.

❖ Strain into a chilled cocktail glass.

4–6 cracked ice cubes
2 measures gin
1 measure triple sec
1 measure lemon juice

Singapore Sling

SERVES 1

10–12 cracked ice cubes
2 measures gin
1 measure cherry brandy
1 measure lemon juice
1 tsp grenadine
soda water, to top up

TO DECORATE

twist of lime rind
cocktail cherries

❖ Put 4–6 of the cracked ice cubes into a cocktail shaker. Pour the gin, cherry brandy, lemon juice and grenadine over the ice. Shake vigorously until a frost forms. ❖ Half fill a chilled highball glass with the remaining cracked ice cubes and strain the cocktail over them. Top up with soda water and decorate with a twist of lime rind and cocktail cherries.

Tom Collins

❖ Put the cracked ice cubes into a cocktail shaker. Pour the gin, lemon juice and Sugar Syrup over the ice. Shake vigorously until a frost forms. ❖ Strain into a tall, chilled tumbler and top up with soda water. Decorate with a slice of lemon and serve with a straw.

SERVES 1

5–6 cracked ice cubes
3 measures gin
2 measures lemon juice
½ measure Sugar Syrup
(see page 9)
soda water, to top up

TO DECORATE
slice of lemon

COCKTAILS

33

Rickey

SERVES 1

4–6 cracked ice cubes
2 measures gin
1 measure lime juice
soda water, to top up

TO DECORATE
slice of lemon

❖ Put the cracked ice cubes into a chilled highball glass or goblet. Pour the gin and lime juice over the ice. Top up with soda water. ❖ Stir gently to mix and decorate with a slice of lemon.

Daiquiri

❖ Put the cracked ice cubes into a cocktail shaker. Pour the rum, lime juice and Sugar Syrup over the ice. Shake vigorously until a frost forms.

❖ Strain into a chilled cocktail glass.

SERVES 1

4–6 cracked ice cubes
2 measures white rum
¾ measure lime juice
½ tsp Sugar Syrup (see page 9)

Shall I compare thee to a summer's day?
Thou art more lovely and more temperate

William Shakespeare *Sonnet 18*

Frozen Daiquiri

SERVES 1

6 crushed ice cubes
2 measures white rum
1 measure lime juice
1 tsp Sugar Syrup (see page 9)

TO DECORATE
slice of lime

❖ Put the crushed ice cubes into a food processor and add the rum, lime juice and Sugar Syrup. Blend until slushy.

❖ Pour into a chilled champagne flute and decorate with a slice of lime.

One swallowe prouveth not
that summer is neare

John Northbrooke *Treatise Against Dancing*

Palm Beach

❖ Put the cracked ice cubes into a cocktail shaker. Pour the rum, gin and pineapple juice over the ice. Shake vigorously until a frost forms. ❖ Strain into a chilled highball glass.

SERVES 1

4–6 cracked ice cubes
1 measure white rum
1 measure gin
1 measure pineapple juice

Piña Colada

SERVES 1

4–6 crushed ice cubes
2 measures white rum
1 measure dark rum
3 measures pineapple juice
2 measures coconut cream

TO DECORATE
wedges of pineapple

❖ Put the crushed ice cubes into a food processor and add the white rum, dark rum, pineapple juice and coconut cream. Blend until smooth.

❖ Pour, without straining, into a tall, chilled glass, decorate with wedges of pineapple speared on a cocktail stick and serve with a straw.

Hayden's Milk Float

❖ Put the cracked ice cubes into a
cocktail shaker. Pour the rum, kirsch,
crème de cacao and cream over the ice.
Shake vigorously until a frost forms.

❖ Strain into a chilled cocktail glass.
Sprinkle with grated chocolate and
decorate with a cocktail cherry.

4–6 cracked ice cubes
2 measures white rum
1 measure kirsch
1 measure white crème
de cacao
1 measure single cream

TO DECORATE
grated chocolate
cocktail cherry

Mai Tai

SERVES 1

4–6 cracked ice cubes
2 measures white rum
2 measures dark rum
1 measure clear Curaçao
1 measure lime juice
1 tbsp orgeat
1 tbsp grenadine

TO DECORATE

paper parasol
slices of pineapple
twist of lime rind
cocktail cherry

❖ Put the cracked ice cubes into a cocktail shaker. Pour the white and dark rums, Curaçao, lime juice, orgeat and grenadine over the ice. Shake vigorously until a frost forms. ❖ Strain into a chilled Collins glass and decorate with the paper parasol, pineapple, twist of lime rind and a cocktail cherry. Serve with straws.

Josiah's Bay Float

❖ Put the cracked ice cubes into a cocktail shaker. Pour the rum, Galliano, pineapple juice, lime juice and Sugar Syrup over the ice. Shake vigorously until a frost forms. ❖ Strain into the pineapple shells, top up with champagne and stir. Decorate with slices of lime and lemon and cocktail cherries. Serve with straws.

SERVES 2

8–10 cracked ice cubes
2 measures golden rum
1 measure Galliano
2 measures pineapple juice
1 measure lime juice
4 tsp Sugar Syrup (see page 9)
champagne, to top up
2 pineapple shells, to serve

TO DECORATE
slices of lime
slices of lemon
cocktail cherries

Planter's Punch

SERVES 1

10–12 cracked ice cubes
dash of grenadine
2 measures white rum
2 measures dark rum
1 measure lemon juice
1 measure lime juice
1 tsp Sugar Syrup (see page 9)
¼ tsp triple sec
sparkling mineral water, to top up

TO DECORATE

slice each of lemon, lime
  and pineapple
cocktail cherry

❖ Put 4–6 of the cracked ice cubes into a cocktail shaker. Dash the grenadine over the ice and pour in the white rum, dark rum, lemon juice, lime juice, Sugar Syrup and triple sec. Shake vigorously until a frost forms. ❖ Half fill a tall, chilled Collins glass with the remaining cracked ice cubes and strain the cocktail over them. Top up with sparkling mineral water and stir gently. Decorate with slices of lemon, lime and pineapple and a cocktail cherry.

Acapulco

❖ Put 4–6 of the cracked ice cubes into a cocktail shaker. Pour the rum, triple sec, lime juice and Sugar Syrup over the ice and add the egg white. Shake vigorously until a frost forms. ❖ Half fill a chilled highball glass with the remaining ice cubes and strain the cocktail over them. Decorate with a sprig of fresh mint.

10–12 cracked ice cubes
2 measures white rum
½ measure triple sec
½ measure lime juice
1 tsp Sugar Syrup (see page 9)
1 egg white

TO DECORATE
sprig of fresh mint

Margarita

SERVES 1

wedge of lime
coarse salt
4–6 cracked ice cubes
3 measures white tequila
1 measure triple sec
2 measures lime juice

TO DECORATE
slice of lime

❖ Rub the rim of a chilled cocktail glass with the lime wedge and then dip in a saucer of coarse salt to frost. ❖ Put the cracked ice cubes into a cocktail shaker. Pour the tequila, triple sec and lime juice over the ice. Shake vigorously until a frost forms. ❖ Strain into the prepared glass and decorate with a slice of lime.

What dreadful hot weather we have!
It keeps me in a continual state of inelegance

Jane Austen *Letter 1796*

Carolina

❖ Put the cracked ice cubes into a cocktail shaker. Pour the tequila, grenadine, vanilla and cream over the ice and add the egg white. Shake vigorously until a frost forms. ❖ Strain into a chilled cocktail glass. Sprinkle with cinnamon and decorate with a cocktail cherry.

SERVES 1

4–6 cracked ice cubes
3 measures golden tequila
1 tsp grenadine
1 tsp vanilla essence
1 measure single cream
1 egg white

TO DECORATE
ground cinnamon
cocktail cherry

Coco Loco

1 coconut

8–10 crushed ice cubes

2 measures white tequila

1 measure gin

1 measure white rum

2 measures pineapple juice

1 tsp Sugar Syrup (see page 9)

½ lime

❖ Carefully saw the top off the coconut, reserving the liquid inside. ❖ Add the crushed ice cubes, tequila, gin, rum, pineapple juice and Sugar Syrup to the coconut, together with the reserved coconut liquid. ❖ Squeeze the lime over the cocktail and drop it in. Stir well and serve with a straw.

Tequila Sunrise

❖ Put the cracked ice cubes into a chilled highball glass. Pour the tequila over the ice and top up with the orange juice. Stir well to mix. ❖ Slowly pour in the grenadine and serve with a straw.

4–6 cracked ice cubes
2 measures white tequila
orange juice, to top up
1 measure grenadine

I have embraced the summer dawn

Arthur Rimbaud *Illuminations*

Long Island Iced Tea

SERVES 1

10–12 cracked ice cubes
2 measures vodka
1 measure gin
1 measure white tequila
1 measure white rum
½ measure white crème
  de menthe
2 measures lemon juice
1 tsp Sugar Syrup (see page 9)
cola, to top up

TO DECORATE
wedge of lime or lemon

❖ Put 4–6 of the cracked ice cubes into a cocktail shaker. Pour the vodka, gin, tequila, rum, crème de menthe, lemon juice and Sugar Syrup over the ice. Shake vigorously until a frost forms. ❖ Half fill a tall, chilled tumbler with the remaining cracked ice cubes and strain the cocktail over them. Top up with cola, decorate with a wedge of lime or lemon and serve with a straw.

Crocodile

❖ Put the cracked ice cubes into a cocktail shaker. Pour the vodka, triple sec, Midori and lemon juice over the ice. Shake vigorously until a frost forms.

❖ Strain into a chilled cocktail glass.

SERVES 1

4–6 cracked ice cubes
2 measures vodka
1 measure triple sec
1 measure Midori
2 measures lemon juice

Cosmopolitan

SERVES 1

4–6 cracked ice cubes
2 measures vodka
½ measure Cointreau
1 measure cranberry juice
juice of ½ lime

TO DECORATE

twist of lime rind
twist of lemon rind

❖ Put the cracked ice cubes into a cocktail shaker. Pour the vodka, Cointreau and cranberry juice over the ice. Add the lime juice and shake well, then strain into a cocktail glass.
❖ Decorate with a twist of lime rind and a twist of lemon rind.

And sing with us, away, Winter away!
Come, Summer, come the sweet seasoun and sun

James I of Scotland *The King is Quair*

Moscow Mule

❖ Put 4–6 of the cracked ice cubes into a cocktail shaker. Pour the vodka and lime juice over the ice. Shake vigorously until a frost forms. ❖ Half fill a chilled highball glass with the remaining cracked ice cubes and strain the cocktail over them. Top up with ginger beer. Decorate with a slice of lime.

SERVES 1

10–12 cracked ice cubes
2 measures vodka
1 measure lime juice
ginger beer, to top up

TO DECORATE
slice of lime

Screwdriver

SERVES 1

6–8 cracked ice cubes
2 measures vodka
orange juice, to top up

TO DECORATE

slice of orange

❖ Fill a chilled highball glass with the cracked ice cubes. Pour the vodka over the ice and top up with orange juice.
❖ Stir well to mix, decorate with a slice of orange and serve with a straw.

John Wood

❖ Put the cracked ice cubes into a cocktail shaker. Dash Angostura bitters over the ice and pour in the vermouth, kümmel, whiskey and lemon juice. Shake vigorously until a frost forms. ❖ Strain into a chilled wine glass.

SERVES 1

4–6 cracked ice cubes
dash of Angostura bitters
2 measures sweet vermouth
½ measure kümmel
½ measure Irish whiskey
1 measure lemon juice

Jade

SERVES 1

4–6 cracked ice cubes
dash of Angostura bitters
¼ measure Midori
¼ measure blue Curaçao
¼ measure lime juice
chilled champagne, to top up

TO DECORATE
slice of lime

❖ Put the cracked ice cubes into a cocktail shaker. Dash Angostura bitters over the ice and pour in the Midori, Curaçao and lime juice. Shake vigorously until a frost forms. ❖ Strain into a chilled champagne flute. Top up with chilled champagne and decorate with a slice of lime.

Sherry Cobbler

❖ Fill a wine glass with the crushed ice cubes. Add the Sugar Syrup and Curaçao and stir until a frost forms. ❖ Pour in the sherry and stir well. Decorate with wedges of pineapple speared on a cocktail stick and a twist of lemon rind.

SERVES 1

6–8 crushed ice cubes
¼ tsp Sugar Syrup (see page 9)
¼ tsp clear Curaçao
4 measures amontillado sherry

TO DECORATE

wedges of pineapple
twist of lemon rind

*No one thinks of winter
when the grass is green!*

Rudyard Kipling *Rewards and Fairies*

Kir

SERVES 1

4–6 crushed ice cubes
2 measures crème de cassis
chilled white wine, to top up

TO DECORATE

twist of lemon rind

❖ Put the crushed ice cubes into a chilled wine glass. Pour the crème de cassis over the ice. ❖ Top up with chilled white wine and stir well. Decorate with a twist of lemon rind.

Buck's Fizz

❖ Pour the champagne into a chilled champagne flute, then pour in the orange juice.

SERVES 1

2 measures chilled champagne
2 measures chilled orange juice

After summer merrily:
Merrily, merrily shall I live now
Under the blossom that hangs on the bough

William Shakespeare *The Tempest*

COCKTAILS

Caribbean Champagne

SERVES 1

½ measure white rum
½ measure crème de bananes
chilled champagne, to top up

TO DECORATE
slices of banana

❖ Pour the rum and crème de bananes into a chilled champagne flute. Top up with champagne. ❖ Stir gently to mix and decorate with slices of banana.

Pimm's No.1

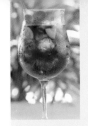

❖ Fill a large glass two-thirds full with
the cracked ice cubes and pour in the
Pimm's. Top up with lemonade and stir
gently. ❖ Decorate with wedges of
cucumber, a sprig of fresh mint and
slices of orange and lemon.

SERVES 1

6–8 cracked ice cubes
1 measure Pimm's No. 1
lemonade, to top up

TO DECORATE
wedges of cucumber
sprig of fresh mint
slices of orange and lemon

milk shakes

Creamy Maple Shake

❖ Pour the milk and maple syrup into a food processor and process gently until combined. ❖ Add the ice cream and almond essence and process until smooth. Pour the mixture into glasses and scatter over the chopped almonds. Add straws and serve.

SERVES 2

150 ml/5 fl oz milk
2 tbsp maple syrup
400 g/14 oz vanilla ice cream
1 tbsp almond essence

TO DECORATE
chopped almonds

Coffee Banana Cooler

SERVES 2

300 ml/10 fl oz milk
4 tbsp instant coffee granules
150 g/5½ oz vanilla ice cream
2 bananas, peeled, sliced
    and frozen

❖ Pour the milk into a food processor, add the coffee granules and process gently until combined. Add half of the vanilla ice cream and process gently, then add the remaining ice cream and process until well combined. ❖ When the mixture is thoroughly blended, add the bananas and process until smooth. Pour the mixture into glasses and serve.

Peppermint Refresher

❖ Pour the milk and peppermint syrup into a food processor and process gently until combined. ❖ Add the peppermint ice cream and process until smooth. Pour the mixture into tall glasses and decorate with sprigs of fresh mint. Add a straw and serve at once.

SERVES 2

150 ml/5 fl oz milk
2 tbsp peppermint syrup
400 g/14 oz peppermint ice cream

TO DECORATE
sprigs of fresh mint

Summer afternoon ... the two most beautiful words in the English language

Henry James *A Backward Glance*

MILK SHAKES

Spiced Banana Milk Shake

SERVES 2

300 ml/10 fl oz milk

½ tsp mixed spice

150 g/5½ oz banana ice cream

2 bananas, peeled, sliced
   and frozen

❖ Pour the milk into a food processor and add the mixed spice. Add half of the banana ice cream and process gently until combined, then add the remaining ice cream and process until well blended. ❖ When the mixture is well combined, add the bananas and process until smooth. Pour the mixture into tall glasses, add straws and serve at once.

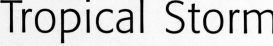

Tropical Storm

❖ Pour the milk and coconut milk into a food processor and process gently until combined. Add half of the ice cream and process gently, then add the remaining ice cream and process until smooth.

❖ Add the bananas and process well, then add the pineapple chunks and pawpaw and process until smooth. Pour the mixture into tall glasses, scatter over the grated coconut and decorate the rims with wedges of pineapple. Serve at once.

SERVES 2

250 ml/9 fl oz milk
50 ml/2 fl oz coconut milk
150 g/5½ oz vanilla ice cream
2 bananas, peeled, sliced
and frozen
200 g/7 oz canned pineapple
chunks, drained
1 pawpaw, peeled, deseeded
and diced

TO DECORATE
grated fresh coconut
wedges of fresh pineapple

Kiwi & Lime Shake

SERVES 2

150 ml/5 fl oz milk
juice of 2 limes
2 kiwi fruit, peeled and chopped
1 tbsp sugar
400 g/14 oz vanilla ice cream

TO DECORATE
slices of kiwi fruit
strips of lime rind

❖ Pour the milk and lime juice into a food processor and process gently until combined. ❖ Add the kiwi fruit and sugar and process gently, then add the ice cream and process until smooth. Pour the mixture into glasses and decorate with slices of kiwi fruit and strips of lime rind. Serve at once.

Mad dogs and Englishmen
Go out in the midday sun
Noël Coward *Mad Dogs and Englishmen*

Peach & Orange Milk Shake

❖ Pour the milk, yogurt and orange juice into a food processor and process gently until combined. ❖ Add the peach slices and crushed ice cubes and process until smooth. Pour the mixture into glasses and decorate with strips of orange rind. Add straws and serve.

100 ml/3 ½ fl oz milk
125 ml/4 fl oz peach yogurt
100 ml/3 ½ fl oz orange juice
225 g/8 oz canned peach slices, drained
6 crushed ice cubes

TO DECORATE

strips of orange rind

Smooth Nectarine Shake

SERVES 2

250 ml/9 fl oz milk
350 g/12 oz lemon sorbet
1 ripe mango, peeled, stoned and diced
2 ripe nectarines, peeled, stoned and diced

❖ Pour the milk into a food processor, add half of the lemon sorbet and process gently until combined. Add the remaining sorbet and process until smooth.

❖ When the mixture is thoroughly blended, gradually add the mango and nectarines and process until smooth. Pour the mixture into glasses, add straws and serve.

Chocolate Milk Shake

❖ Pour the milk and chocolate syrup into a food processor and process gently until combined. ❖ Add the chocolate ice cream and process until smooth. Pour the mixture into tall glasses and scatter over the grated chocolate. Serve at once.

SERVES 2

150 ml/5 fl oz milk
2 tbsp chocolate syrup
400 g/14 oz chocolate
ice cream

TO DECORATE
grated chocolate

For him in vain the envious seasons roll
Who bears eternal summer in his soul

Oliver Wendell Holmes *The Old Player*

thirst quenchers

Sparkling Peach Melba

❖ Rub the raspberries through a nylon sieve with the back of a wooden spoon, then transfer the purée to a cocktail shaker with the ice cubes. ❖ Pour the peach juice into the cocktail shaker and shake vigorously until a frost forms. ❖ Strain into a tall, chilled tumbler and top up with sparkling mineral water. Stir gently, add straws and serve.

SERVES 1

60 g/2¼ oz frozen raspberries
6–8 cracked ice cubes
4 measures peach juice
sparkling mineral water,
to top up

Island Cooler

SERVES 1

8–10 cracked ice cubes
2 measures orange juice
1 measure lemon juice
1 measure pineapple juice
1 measure pawpaw juice
½ tsp grenadine
sparkling mineral water,
  to top up

TO DECORATE
wedge of pineapple
cocktail cherry

❖ Put 4–6 of the cracked ice cubes into a cocktail shaker. Pour the orange juice, lemon juice, pineapple juice, pawpaw juice and grenadine over the ice. Shake vigorously until a frost forms. ❖ Half fill a chilled Collins glass with the remaining cracked ice cubes and pour the cocktail over them. Top up with sparkling mineral water and stir gently. Decorate with a wedge of pineapple and a cocktail cherry speared on a cocktail stick.

Italian Soda

❖ Fill a chilled Collins glass with the cracked ice cubes. Pour the hazelnut syrup over the ice and top up with sparkling mineral water. ❖ Stir gently and decorate with a slice of lime.

SERVES 1

6–8 cracked ice cubes
1–1½ measures
hazelnut syrup
sparkling mineral water,
to top up

TO DECORATE
slice of lime

In winter I get up at night
And dress by yellow candle-light.
In summer, quite the other way,
I have to go to bed by day

Robert Louis Stevenson, *Bed in Summer*

Lime & Lemon Grass Cooler

SERVES 4

egg white and caster sugar,
  to frost
2 limes, peeled and each cut
  into 8 pieces
1 small lemon grass stalk,
  roughly chopped
3 tbsp caster sugar
4 crushed ice cubes
125 ml/4 fl oz water
4 slices of lime
soda water, to top up

❖ To frost the rim of the glasses, pour a little egg white into a saucer. Dip the rim of each glass briefly into the egg white and then into a saucer of the sugar.

❖ Place the lime pieces and lemon grass in a food processor with the sugar and crushed ice cubes. ❖ Add the water and process for a few seconds, but not until completely smooth. ❖ Strain the mixture into the frosted glasses. Add a slice of lime to each glass and top up to taste with soda water. Serve at once.

Shirley Temple

* Put 4–6 of the cracked ice cubes into a cocktail shaker. Pour the lemon juice, grenadine and Sugar Syrup over the ice and shake vigorously. * Half fill a small, chilled glass with the remaining ice cubes and strain the cocktail over them. Top up with ginger ale. Decorate with a slice of orange and a cocktail cherry.

SERVES 1

8–10 cracked ice cubes
2 measures lemon juice
½ measure grenadine
½ measure Sugar Syrup
(see page 9)
ginger ale, to top up

TO DECORATE
slice of orange
cocktail cherry

Faux Kir

SERVES 1

1 measure chilled
  raspberry syrup
chilled white grape juice,
  to top up

TO DECORATE

twist of lemon rind

❖ Pour the raspberry syrup into a chilled
wine glass. Top up with the grape juice.

❖ Stir well to mix and decorate with a
twist of lemon rind.

*I know I am but summer to your heart,
   And not the full four seasons of the year*

Edna St Vincent Millay *I Know I Am But Summer*

Soft Sangria

❖ Put the grape juice, orange juice, cranberry juice, lemon juice, lime juice and Sugar Syrup into a chilled punch bowl and stir well. ❖ Add the ice and decorate with the slices of lemon, orange and lime.

SERVES 20

1.5 litres/2¾ pints
red grape juice
300 ml/10 fl oz orange juice
3 measures cranberry juice
2 measures lemon juice
2 measures lime juice
4 measures Sugar Syrup
(see page 9)
block of ice

TO DECORATE
slices of lemon
slices of orange
slices of lime

Iced Coffee & Mint Slush

SERVES 2

400 ml/14 fl oz milk

200 ml/7 fl oz coffee syrup

100 ml/3½ fl oz peppermint
 syrup

1 tbsp chopped fresh mint
 leaves

4 crushed ice cubes

TO DECORATE

grated chocolate

sprigs of fresh mint

❖ Pour the milk, coffee syrup and peppermint syrup into a food processor and process gently until combined. ❖ Add the mint and crushed ice cubes and process until a slushy consistency has been reached. ❖ Pour the mixture into glasses. Scatter over the grated chocolate, decorate with sprigs of fresh mint and serve.

Mocha Cream

❖ Put the milk, cream and sugar into a food processor and process gently until combined. ❖ Add the cocoa powder and coffee syrup or granules and process well, then add the crushed ice cubes and process until smooth. ❖ Pour the mixture into glasses. Top with whipped cream, scatter over the grated chocolate and serve.

SERVES 2

200 ml/7 fl oz milk
50 ml/2 fl oz single cream
1 tbsp brown sugar
2 tbsp cocoa powder
1 tbsp coffee syrup or instant coffee granules
6 crushed ice cubes

TO DECORATE

whipped cream
grated chocolate

Coffee Hazelnut Slush

250 ml/9 fl oz water
3 tbsp instant coffee granules
125 ml/4 fl oz sparkling water
1 tbsp hazelnut syrup
2 tbsp brown sugar
6 crushed ice cubes

TO DECORATE
slices of lime or lemon

❖ Use the water and coffee granules to brew some hot coffee, then leave to cool to room temperature. Transfer to a jug, cover with clingfilm and chill in the refrigerator for at least 45 minutes.
❖ When the coffee has chilled, pour it into a food processor. Add the sparkling water, hazelnut syrup and sugar and process well. Add the crushed ice cubes and process until smooth. ❖ Pour the mixture into glasses, decorate the rims with slices of lime or lemon and serve.

Iced Coffee with Cream

❖ Use the water and coffee granules to brew some hot coffee, then leave to cool to room temperature. Transfer to a jug, cover with clingfilm and chill in the refrigerator for at least 45 minutes. ❖ When the coffee has chilled, pour it into a food processor. Add the sugar and process until well combined. Add the crushed ice cubes and process until smooth. ❖ Pour the mixture into glasses. Float single cream on the top, decorate with whole coffee beans and serve.

SERVES 2

400 ml/14 fl oz water
2 tbsp instant coffee granules
2 tbsp brown sugar
6 crushed ice cubes

TO DECORATE
single cream
whole coffee beans

Spiced Lemon Tea

SERVES 2

400 ml/14 fl oz water
4 cloves
1 small cinnamon stick
2 tea bags
3–4 tbsp lemon juice
1–2 tbsp brown sugar

TO DECORATE
slices of lemon

❖ Put the water, cloves and cinnamon into a saucepan and bring to the boil. Remove from the heat and add the tea bags. Leave to infuse for 5 minutes, then remove the tea bags. ❖ Stir in the lemon juice and sugar to taste. Return the pan to the heat and warm through gently.
❖ Remove the pan from the heat and strain the tea into heatproof glasses. Decorate with slices of lemon and serve.

Classic Iced Tea

❖ Put the tea bags, mint leaves and sugar in a heatproof bowl. Pour in the boiling water and stir well. Leave to stand for 15 minutes. ❖ Strain the mixture into a jug, leave to cool, then chill for at least 1 hour. ❖ Put the ice cubes into tall glasses and pour over the tea. Decorate with sprigs of fresh mint.

SERVES 6

6 Chinese green tea bags
140 g/5 oz fresh mint leaves
4 tbsp sugar
1.5 litres/2¾ pints boiling water

TO DECORATE
ice cubes
sprigs of fresh mint

*And you shall wander hand in hand
with Love in summer's wonderland*

Alfred Noyes *The Barrel-Organ*

Iced Citrus Tea

300 ml/10 fl oz water
2 tea bags
100 ml/3½ fl oz orange juice
4 tbsp lime juice
1–2 tbsp brown sugar
8 ice cubes

TO DECORATE
wedge of lime
granulated sugar
slices of orange, lemon or lime

❖ Bring the water to the boil in a saucepan. Remove from the heat, add the tea bags and leave to infuse for 5 minutes. Remove the tea bags and leave to cool to room temperature. Transfer to a jug, cover and leave to chill in the fridge for 45 minutes. ❖ Once chilled, pour in the fruit juices. Add sugar to taste. ❖ Rub the glasses' rims with a wedge of lime. Dip them in a saucer of sugar to frost. Put the ice cubes into the glasses and pour over the tea. Decorate with slices of orange, lemon or lime.

Elderflower & Pear Smoothie

❖ Peel and quarter the pears, discarding the cores. Place in a saucepan with the elderflowers, strip of lemon rind, sugar and water. Cover tightly and simmer until the pears are very soft. Leave to cool. ❖ Discard the elderflowers and lemon rind. Put the pears, cooking liquid and milk into a food processor and process until smooth. ❖ Serve immediately with the langues de chat biscuits.

SERVES 2

4 small firm pears
2 elderflower heads, freshly picked
1 strip of lemon rind
1 tbsp soft brown sugar
4 tbsp water
200 ml/7 fl oz semi-skimmed milk

TO SERVE

langues de chat biscuits

Raspberry & Apple Quencher

SERVES 2

8 crushed ice cubes
2 tbsp raspberry syrup
500 ml/18 fl oz chilled
  apple juice

TO DECORATE
whole raspberries
pieces of apple

❖ Divide the crushed ice cubes between the glasses and pour over the raspberry syrup. ❖ Top up each glass with chilled apple juice and stir well. Decorate with the whole raspberries and pieces of apple on cocktail sticks and serve.

Summer has set in with its usual severity

Samuel Taylor Coleridge *Letters of Charles Lamb*

Christmas in Summer

❖ Ensure that you use glasses that are suitable for holding boiling water. ❖ Divide the cranberry cordial between the glasses, then add a crushed allspice berry, an orange slice and a cinnamon stick to each glass. ❖ Pour the boiling water into the glasses. Leave to cool, then chill. ❖ When you are ready to serve, float a scoop of ice cream on the top of each glass.

SERVES 2

75 ml/2½ fl oz cranberry cordial
2 allspice berries, crushed
2 slices of orange
2 cinnamon sticks
250 ml/9 fl oz boiling water
2 scoops of luxury vanilla
ice cream

Strawberries & Cream

SERVES 2

150 g/5½ oz frozen strawberries

100 ml/3½ fl oz single cream

200 ml/7 fl oz cold
 full-cream milk

1 tbsp caster sugar

TO DECORATE

few borage flowers

❖ Put the strawberries, cream, milk and caster sugar into a food processor and process until smooth. ❖ Pour into glasses, decorate with borage flowers and serve.

Carrot & Orange Cream

❖ Pour the carrot juice and orange juice into a food processor and process gently until well combined. Add the ice cream and process until thoroughly blended.

❖ Add the crushed ice cubes and process until smooth. Pour the mixture into glasses, decorate with slices of orange and strips of orange rind and serve.

SERVES 2

175 ml/6 fl oz carrot juice
175 ml/6 fl oz orange juice
150 g/5½ oz vanilla ice cream
6 crushed ice cubes

TO DECORATE
slices of orange
strips of orange rind

Lassi

SERVES 2

100 ml/3½ fl oz natural yogurt
500 ml/18 fl oz milk
1 tbsp rosewater
3 tbsp honey
1 ripe mango, peeled, stoned
  and diced
6 crushed ice cubes

TO DECORATE

edible rose petals, optional

❖ Pour the yogurt and milk into a food processor and process gently until combined. ❖ Add the rosewater and honey and process until thoroughly blended, then add the mango along with the crushed ice cubes and process until smooth. Pour the mixture into glasses, decorate with edible rose petals, if using, and serve.

Cherry Soda

❖ Divide the crushed ice cubes between
the glasses and pour over the cherry
syrup. ❖ Top up each glass with sparkling
water. Decorate with maraschino cherries
speared on cocktail sticks and serve.

SERVES 2

8 crushed ice cubes
2 tbsp cherry syrup
500 ml/18 fl oz sparkling water

TO DECORATE
maraschino cherries

That thou, light-winged Dryad of the trees,
In some melodious plot
Of beechen green, and shadows numberless,
Singest of summer in full-throated ease

John Keats *Ode to a Nightingale*

Home-made Lemonade

SERVES 2

150 ml/5 fl oz water
6 tbsp sugar
1 tsp grated lemon rind
125 ml/4 fl oz lemon juice
6 ice cubes
sparkling water, to top up

TO DECORATE

wedge of lemon
granulated sugar
slices of lemon

❖ Put the water, sugar and lemon rind into a saucepan and bring to the boil, stirring constantly. Continue to boil, stirring, for 5 minutes. ❖ Remove and leave to cool. Stir in the juice, then transfer to a jug, cover and chill for at least 2 hours. ❖ To serve, rub the rims of the glasses with a wedge of lemon, then dip them in a saucer of sugar to frost. Put the ice cubes into the glasses. ❖ Pour the syrup over the ice to quarter-fill the glasses and top up with sparkling water. Stir and decorate with slices of lemon.

Traditional Ginger Beer

❖ Thinly peel the lemon rind with a vegetable peeler. Squeeze the juice.
❖ Put the ginger, sugar, cream of tartar and lemon rind into a heatproof bowl and add the boiling water, stirring to dissolve the sugar. Leave to cool. ❖ Add the lemon juice and yeast, cover with clingfilm and leave at room temperature for 3 days. Skim off any scum, then siphon into strong, sterilized bottles. Seal and store for 3 days before drinking.

MAKES 4.5 LITRES/8 PINTS

2 large lemons
55 g/2 oz fresh root ginger, peeled and bruised
450 g/1 lb sugar
15 g/½ oz cream of tartar
4.5 litres/8 pints boiling water
1 tsp dried yeast

Pineapple Float

175 ml/6 fl oz pineapple juice
90 ml/3¼ fl oz coconut milk
200 g/7 oz vanilla ice cream
140 g/5 oz frozen pineapple
  chunks
175 ml/6 fl oz sparkling water

TO SERVE

2 pineapple shells, optional

❖ Pour the pineapple juice and coconut milk into a food processor. Add the ice cream and process until smooth.

❖ Add the pineapple chunks and process well. Pour the mixture into scooped-out pineapple shells or tall glasses until two-thirds full. Top up with the sparkling water, add straws and serve.

All the live murmur of a summer's day

Matthew Arnold *The Scholar-Gipsy*

Pomegranate Passion

❖ Cut the pomegranates in half and extract the juice with an old-fashioned lemon squeezer. ❖ Halve the passion fruit and sieve the pulp into a bowl. Mix in the pomegranate juice and honey. ❖ Put the cracked ice cubes into the glasses, pour over the juices and serve.

SERVES 2

2 ripe pomegranates
1 passion fruit
1 tbsp clear honey
cracked ice cubes

Index